Meeting special needs

a practical guide to support children with
Speech, Language and Communication Needs (SLCN)

by Mary Mountstephen

Acknowledgements

To my family with love and thanks for their support and patience.

Also, with grateful thanks to Pippa Counsell, Speech, Language and Communication Therapist and Marlene Rattigan for her lovely 'kidz-fiz-biz' activities.

Note on Terms used in the book

Throughout this book the term practitioners is used to include all play workers, child minders and childcare workers.

The term 'setting' applies to wherever the play/ childcare takes place.

The terms 'parent/carer are used interchangeably in most contexts as are the terms he/ his/ she/ hers.

The term 'special educational needs' has a legal definition. Children with **special educational needs** all have **learning difficulties** or **disabilities** that make it harder for them to learn than most children of the same age. These children may need extra or different help from that given to other children of the same age'. (DCSF 2008)

The term Speech, Language and Communication Needs will be referred to by its abbreviation: SLCN

Published by Practical Pre-School Books
St Jude's Church, Dulwich Road, Herne Hill, London, SE24 0PB Tel. 020 7738 5454
© MA Education 2010 www.practicalpreschoolbooks.com

Meeting special needs: a practical guide to support children with Speech, Language and Communication Needs (SLCN) ISBN: 978-1-904-575-96-2

Contents

Preface

Erin

Erin is just two years old and communicates very little to anyone in the setting, although her parents say she talks with them in the home. In the setting, she needs to concentrate very hard to follow spoken language and this is difficult if there is background noise and the instructions are not being given individually to her.

Group activities present problems for her if she is struggling to follow what is going on and can't take part. Her mother says things are better if she is encouraged to feel relaxed, as when she becomes anxious or withdrawn, her communication difficulties will feel and appear more pronounced.

When she is at home or in her nursery, Erin needs sensitive encouragement to ask and answer questions with an adult or another child.

An adult might say: 'I never know what Erin wants, she just points at things and cries when we don't understand her. She's always playing on her own'.

Erin might be feeling: frustrated, angry, emotional and frightened.

Her parent says: 'She's so shy; she never speaks to anyone... I just want to stop her clinging to me all the time'.

The focus of this book is on helping you to identify what it is that Erin, for example, is finding hard to do and then to use your observations and discussions to find ways of supporting her so that she can flourish and thrive to the best of her ability. If she can be prevented from experiencing repeated failure, she is more likely to develop resilience and the self-confidence to try new activities. We know that the early years are a very important time for physical, emotional, intellectual and social development, and both positive and negative experiences can have a profound influence on later learning and development.

This guide is not intended to cover all aspects of these difficulties, but it will give you a greater understanding of how speech, language and communication develop, as well as offering guidelines for support and signposts to further reading, professional development and useful resources.

Introduction

When a child seems to be falling behind others in their rate of early development, this can be a cause for worry and concern at home, at play and in early years settings. In the pre-school setting, you may be working with a child who has problems with their movement, social interaction or play skills and you may be looking for reasons to explain this and for advice on what you can do and how you can support both the child and his family. You may feel reluctant to discuss this with colleagues or parents if you feel they may not share your perceptions. However, a practitioner is not there to diagnose but to observe and identify where a child may be experiencing difficulties and to put strategies in place to support the child. If concerns still persist after a period of time, referral to a specialist should be considered and discussed.

> Communication is fundamental for learning and development. Children and young people with a communication disability cannot express themselves, understand others or build relationships because of problems with language or communication. One in ten children and young people struggle with this invisible disability. Without the right help, at the right time, they will be left out and left behind. (I CAN www.ican.org.uk)

Many practitioners have concerns about children's speech, language and communication skills and this book aims to support you in the early identification of difficulties and in providing early support.

Speech and language difficulties account for one of the largest groups of young children needing support. In any Reception or Key Stage 1 classroom in the UK at least 10 per cent of children are likely to have significant difficulties in one or both areas. Some children start school with the speech and language levels of two-year-olds and there are an increasing number of children who have missed the concentrated language input provided by parents and carers which focuses on the child's play and interests. In primary schools, it is worthwhile noting that SLCN represent the most prevalent type of special educational need (23%) amongst pupils with statements of SEN, according to the I CAN publication, *Speech, Language and Communication Needs and Primary School-Aged Children* (I Can talk series). Issue 6.

with special educational needs (SEN). This is a four year programme covering the period 2008-2011 which will provide support for leadership teams, teachers and practitioners working with children with a range of special educational needs of all ages. The EYFS Inclusion Development Programme for Speech, Language and Communication Needs (SLCN) aims to help teachers and practitioners to develop their own skills in the identification of speech, language and communication needs and how to support them. It has identified that in some areas more than 50% of children enter school with 'transient' language communication difficulties. This refers to difficulties which are 'not lasting or remaining' and children are likely to catch up given the right support. Children with more persistent difficulties however will need differentiated support to reach the goals outlined in Every Child Matters. The resources are organized according to the four sections of the EYFS (A Unique Child, Positive Relationships, Enabling Environments, and Learning and Development). There are many resources available to help early years' practitioners in schools and settings in the early identification and support of children with speech, language and communication needs. To get the best from the resources it is recommended that colleagues work together, but you can also work through the materials on your own. You will learn more about:

- children's language development

- how to identify children with particular needs

- best practice for children with SLCN

- effective ways to interact with children, parents and other professionals

- developing inclusive practice

(Source: (2008) *Inclusion Development Programme Supporting Children with Speech, Language and Communication Needs: Guidance for Practitioners in the Early Years Foundation Stage*. DCSF ref:00215-2008BKT-EN)

The Inclusion Development Programme

The Inclusion Development Programme (IDP) is part of the Government's strategy for including children

Some Indicators of Speech, Language and Communication Difficulties

Are you concerned about a child you know and observe who has a persistent combination or cluster of the difficulties below?

- The child's language sounds immature: may says phrases like 'Me do that' for much longer than you would expect

- Talks hesitantly with words pronounced incorrectly, uses simple sounds to replace more difficult ones

- Difficulty naming words, wrong choice of words

- Use of pointing, grunting and gesture as opposed to speech

- Problems with eating, drinking and swallowing

- Difficulty learning new vocabulary

- Looks blank when spoken to

- Poor listening skills

- Watches to see what other children are doing and seems hesitant to follow instructions

- May have social difficulties in relating to other children and may be prone to tantrums because of frustration

Parents may be told that their child who seems to be delayed in their development, according to developmental milestones, will usually catch up in their own time. This is true in some cases; however we know that not every child moves forward at the same pace or demonstrates new skills at the same time as other children around them. Development may be more advanced in some areas than others, and this can be confusing when trying to establish if there really is a problem.

Differences in Development in Boys and Girls

It is important to note that in general boys' language development can be slower than that of girls. This is said to relate to the relative immaturity of the male nervous system at birth. However, there may be other reasons why boys' language development appears to lag behind that of girls.

The University of Michigan's Department of Psychology cites evidence that girls start to talk before boys and also tend to have a higher vocabulary and make more two-word utterances. This is said to be because of the changes that take place in learning happen earlier for girls (between 14 and 20 months of age) than for boys (20–24 months of age). Some research has also shown that fathers will play more rough and tumble games with boys, while fathers are more likely to focus on different kinds of interactions and communication with their daughters.

Thinking Point

- What other reasons might there be for boys' language development and communication seeming to be less advanced than girls?

- Do you agree with the statements above?

- What effect might there be when there is a younger child in the family whose older sibling says everything for them?

What are the implications of this?

Boys may be assessed as being less able, when they are actually absorbed in other ways of exploring activities.

Boys may not be considered 'at risk' of communication difficulties until later, less likely to receive early intervention.

Adults may provide girls with explanations for events, instead of encouraging them to explore first hand through play.

Some children who begin in the setting with an apparent delay in the development of their skills quickly make progress as they are included in language rich activities. Others may be less forthcoming and need support to become more confident.

Note: These are broad statements which will not apply to all children: there will be boys who excel at language early on and girls who do not. The expectations of the setting and the child's cultural heritage can also have some influence on this.

However, when a child seems to have a cluster of ongoing challenges which are affecting their day to day living, steps need to be taken. It becomes increasingly important to identify areas of strength and areas which are most in need of targeted support and to put into place strategies to support firm foundations for learning and living.

Bilingualism

There may be many advantages to being exposed to more than one language from birth, including, for example, positive self-esteem and attitudes towards language learning, learning flexibility and increased problem-solving.

Some children who have English as an additional language may also have speech, language or communication difficulties; however it is important that practitioners recognize that a child must not be regarded as having a learning difficulty solely because their home language is different from the language in which they will be taught.

When children mix words from both languages in their early years, it should be seen not as an indicator of confusion, but as an indicator of how children can make choices about how to express themselves most fluently. Young children (and many adults) think in their first language and they need to be able to practice this in the early years' setting as well as being given direct support for their language development.

Meeting Special Educational Needs

The Special Educational Needs Code of Practice gives guidance to early education settings and it sets out the procedures that must be followed. It places great emphasis on the early identification of special educational needs so that children can be helped as quickly as possible. It recognizes that children learn in different ways and that their needs should be met within a mainstream setting as far as possible. All children should have access to a broad balanced and relevant curriculum and the views of the parents and child (wherever possible) should be taken into account.

An important point to bear in mind is that the identification of, planning for, and working with, children with special needs is the responsibility of all staff.

> ### Thinking Point
>
> Try to think of three ways to improve the way in which your setting demonstrates respect for the languages of bilingual children. Do they feel that their home language is valued and respected? How would you know?

What is Communication Delay?

I CAN, a charity helping children with speech and language difficulties, has created the following communication disability definition:

Communication is fundamental for learning and development. Children and young people with a communication disability cannot express themselves, understand others or build relationships because of problems in one or more of these areas:

- Understanding and finding the right words.

- Producing, ordering and discriminating between speech sounds.

- Using rules about how words, phrases and sentences are formed to convey meaning.

- Using and understanding language in different social contexts. One in ten children and young people struggle with this invisible disability. Without the right help, at the right time, they will be left out and left behind. (www.ican.org.uk)

What are "SLCN"?

- Problems with forming sounds and words.

- Problems with formulating sentences and expressing ideas.

- Problems with understanding speech and language.

- Problems using language socially.

- Delays and disorders in the development of speech and language skills.

When do SLCN become apparent?

The majority of SLCN are identifiable from the second year of life. Some children have problems that are specifically about speech and language. Some children have problems related to other conditions that affect speech and language. Some children will have difficulties in some of these areas, but not in others. For example, they may have difficulty in speaking words clearly (in the articulation of words), but they have no difficulty in understanding words, expressing themselves or interacting with others.

Specific Language Impairment

SLI is diagnosed when a child has selective difficulties in mastering language, but is developing normally in other respects. They generally have normal hearing, age-appropriate scores on tests of non-verbal intelligence and no evidence of neurological damage. Their physical development may also be normal.

Research indicates that if a child who experiences difficulties in these areas has their needs recognized early and interventions are put in place there is a strong likelihood that speedy progress and improvements can be made (Dukes and Smith 2009).

What are the most common communication problems in children?

Speech/Articulation problems

This is a difficulty with pronouncing sounds to make words. There are many reasons children have difficulty in making sounds. These include hearing problems, poor muscle control of the tongue, lips, teeth and mouth, cleft palate or learning problems. However, often there is no apparent reason for the problem.

Language problems

Expressive: what the child says.

Expressive language is generally seen as consisting of three parts:

- Expressive vocabulary

- Word and sentence formation

- Pragmatic development: the ability to use language socially

Expressive language difficulties can show up in problems with grammar, as in "Him is mean," or vocabulary such as calling a "lion", a "tiger". Expressive language relates to how you convey meaning to others using spoken language or non-verbal language such as gestures, facial expression, sign language and body language. It refers to having the words to describe objects, actions and feelings and being able to use these words in sentences and conversations, following the rules of grammar. A child might point or make noises instead of using words. An older child may use single words rather than sentences.

Receptive: what the child understands.

Receptive language develops as the child grows and is able to understand more complex communications. Receptive language is seen as the foundation for all language and communication skills and it continues to develop into Key Stage 1 and beyond.

Receptive problems can show up in misunderstanding what is being said to you, including difficulty following instructions or answering questions strangely - for example, answering "What do you do at night?" with "Pyjamas". The ability to process language and to make sense of what people are saying is fundamental to our ability to understand our world and interact with it meaningfully.

It is important to remember that receptive language skills develop before expressive language skills and that many skills must be developed in order that a child can express themselves and understand others. Many children who have a language delay or language disorder may have a great difference between their ability to understand language and to use language socially. This can be a great source of frustration for them. Appropriate attention and listening skills need to be in place to support the development of age-appropriate, receptive language skills.

Communication

This can take place with or without words and includes how we relate to those around us. As children mature, communication means the ability to use language in different ways: to question, clarify, describe and debate. Communication also means using the non-verbal elements of communication, such as the conventions of good listening, looking at people when talking to them, knowing how to take turns in conversations and debates, and how to adapt our language according to the person we are speaking to, or the situation we find ourselves in.

Structure of language: some useful terms

Phonology: The sounds of language.

Grammar: The rules of language structure: how words are assembled.

Vocabulary: The collection of words an individual understands and may (or may not) be able to pronounce and use.

Pragmatics: The way we understand and use language and communication in social situations, including non-verbal aspects such as body language, our expressions, and how we engage in conversation and turn taking.

Fluency disorders (stuttering)

With this type of problem, the child has difficulty with the flow or rhythm of speech. The smooth flow of speech can be interrupted in a number of ways: repeating sounds, syllables, words and phrases, prolonging sounds, or using interjections such as "urm." Stuttering is a feature of typically developing speech and it is quite normal for some children between two and a half years and five years of age to go through phases of hesitations and repetitions. However, it is recommended that parents should discuss this with their GP if they are concerned or anxious or if the child is showing frustration, avoiding conversation, or if any of the following apply:

• There is a family history of stuttering.

• The child shows signs of struggle when trying to get the words out, for example: stamping feet, grimacing, fist clenching.

• Stuttering lasts for longer than two months.

• The child shows signs of anxiety or frustration about speech.

• The length of each block, hesitation or repetition is more than just a fleeting moment.

(Source: Kidshealth: New Zealand)

Verbal Dyspraxia

Children with verbal dyspraxia have difficulty in making and coordinating the precise movements of the speech muscles necessary for clear speech. There is no damage to muscles or nerves: it is a speech problem. They have difficulty in:

• Making speech sounds.

• Sequencing sounds to make up a word.

• Keeping speech clear in longer sentences.

• Controlling speed, rhythm, loudness of the voice.

• Expressing themselves through language, but normal or above average receptive language skills.

• Their speech develops slowly in the first few years.

These children may want to communicate but are unable to do so effectively.

What Might Cause Speech, Language and Communication Needs?

There may be a number of reasons why a child is showing signs of delay in their speech, language or communication development.

One possible cause identified in the Inclusion Development Plan is:

• Ear infections
Children who have suffered hearing loss through repeated ear infections are likely to have missed out in terms of their access to listening and interacting effectively. The process of listening, concentrating and interpreting can be a tiring and frustrating experience as the child misses out on parts of conversations, sentences and words. For some children, repeated ear infections can persist for years, placing an increasing strain on the child's ability to function effectively in many aspects of their day to day life. Repeated ear infections can have a longer term impact than just the period of infection. Although children may catch up, they are more likely to have delayed auditory processing skills such as following instructions. They may pass a hearing test, carried out in quiet surroundings on a one to one basis, but struggle to hear and understand spoken information in the setting and a home. Background noise intensifies the problem.

Glue Ear sometimes develops after a cough, cold or ear infection when extra mucus is made; however, in many cases it does not begin with an ear infection. It has been claimed that more than seven out of ten children have at least one episode of glue ear before they are four years old. In most cases, it only lasts a short time, however Dr Lindsay Peer (2005) in her book *Glue Ear: An Essential Guide for Teachers, Parents and Health Professionals* believes that the existence of Glue Ear in early childhood has a major impact upon the development of language and literacy as well as on the emotional stability of the individual. She refers to the long term impact on these skills, many years after levels of hearing have returned to within normal limits.

Indicators of glue ear include earache, frequent colds, waking at night, breathing through the mouth, hearing difficulties, seeming to ignore instructions, frustration and poor social interaction.

Other possible causes of SLCN include:

• Difficulties in using oral muscles effectively: for example in cerebral palsy.

• Family history or a family related condition.

- Sensory processing problems: A child with sensory processing problems can become quickly overloaded by what is going on around them. Their way of coping may include switching off.

- Problems in pregnancy or birth which may affect the developing brain and be part of a more global developmental delay.

- A recognized syndrome or disorder that is associated with communication difficulties such as semantic pragmatic disorder, Asperger Syndrome and selective mutism or foetal alcohol syndrome. The difficulties in communication and language seen in children with autism may be observed in toddlers or babies who are unresponsive and can appear to be deaf. (Although children who are deaf may also, although rarely, show signs of autism). Autistic children will often take people's hands directly to what they want rather than communicating their needs. When their speech develops, it very often sounds stilted, with a monotonous drone or an odd 'sing-song' manner.

- A lack of stimulation and support in terms of access to rich language experiences, which contribute to the development of appropriate speech, language and communication skills.

In many cases, it is not possible to determine the cause of the difficulty as there may be overlapping reasons and a number of differing factors that combine together to influence the child's development.

Some of the skills which are important if a child is to develop language include:

- The ability to pay attention to visual and auditory information: Does the child seem able to sustain even short periods of attention: are they aware of what is going on around them?

- The ability to imitate gestures and sounds: Do they understand what they need to do and can they physically copy movements?

- The ability to take turns: To communicate with others, we need to know when it is our turn to listen and when to speak.

Who to ask for advice and support

Health Visitors

Health Visitors are an excellent source of information, support and guidance. They are specially trained nurses who work with children, families and communities. They focus mainly on families with children aged under five and provide advice and support on the following:

- Feeding, safety, physical and emotional development as well as behaviour management, sleep management, diet, breast feeding support, minor ailments, safety, immunisations and general child development.

- Services and support for families in special circumstances, e.g. homelessness, domestic violence, travelling families, older people, families who have lost a child through sudden infant death syndrome (cot death), and children with special needs.

(Source: NHS Careers web-site: www.nhscareers. nhs.uk)

Speech and Language Therapists

The role of a Speech and Language Therapist (SLT) is to assess and treat speech, language and communication problems in people of all ages to enable them to communicate to the best of their ability. They may also work with people who have eating and swallowing problems.

Speech and Language Therapists work closely with teachers and other health professionals including doctors, nurses and psychologists.

SLTs help children and adults who have the following types of problems:

- Difficulty producing and using speech

- Difficulty understanding language

- Difficulty using language

- Difficulty with feeding, chewing or swallowing

- A stammer

- A voice problem

Many children with speech, language and communication difficulties or delays will make good progress within the setting, given time. The Inclusion Development Plan identifies a 'window of opportunity' in relation to a child's development and states that support may be required over a two year period if a child with difficulties is to reach a level similar to his peers by the age of five and a half. If this is achieved, it is considered that their prospects will be 'considerably better'. However, a minority of children will need the support of a Speech and Language Therapist (SLT), or other types of specialist support such as hearing impairment support. A SLT may work with groups or individually, as well as either directly with the child or indirectly by offering training to the parents or other adults working with the child.

When to seek support

Parents or carers have the right to contact speech and language therapy services directly through the NHS Trust. There is no lower age limit for referring children for speech and language therapy assessment and some children with complex needs will have been receiving support since shortly after birth. Services will vary though in the age at which they will accept referrals.

Occupational Therapists

Occupational Therapists work with young children, adolescents, adults and older people in these areas:

- physical rehabilitation

- mental health services

- learning disability

- primary care

- paediatrics

- environmental adaptation

- care management

- equipment for daily living

(Source: www.nhscareers.nhs.uk)

A Paediatric Occupational Therapist works with children to make the most of their potential ability in specific areas and to increase their independence at home, in school and in their social activities. Many children, for a range of reasons, are not able to participate successfully in meaningful activities. Occupational Therapists may become involved with a child to help them develop skills so that they can, with practice, participate more fully. The therapist will usually ask how the child and the family see the problem and talk with other professionals who know the child (such as the early years practitioner). Specific activities and formal assessments are then carried out to define the exact nature of the problem. This may include observations, interviews and standardized assessments. The therapist will then give advice on strategies and ways of overcoming problems. Whenever possible the emphasis is on learning through play activities which will motivate the child.

A therapist may work on co-ordination, concentration and attention, emotional well-being, self-esteem and coping skills, or fine motor skills.

What does this mean for the child?

Human beings communicate in numerous ways, and language forms only a small percentage of interaction. Children are keen observers of all forms of communication so as to make sense of what is going on and to be able to take part. Practitioners need to reflect on their observations of the children's communications and on their own ability to nurture good communication skills in all children, particularly those who might be unwilling or unable to communicate effectively.

Two year olds are definitely capable of being skillful communicators. But by this age it is possible to notice the impact of their early experiences. Young children need plenty of relaxed opportunities to talk as well as listen. Their language skills, as well as general learning, will be stunted if adults see communication mainly as 'I talk –you listen' or 'My questions are more important than yours.' (Lindon J (2008), *What Does It Mean to be Two (Revised Edition)*. Step Forward Publishing)

Erin will learn about people, communication and relating to others by observing the adults around her.

We cannot 'not' communicate. We do it by our presence and by our absence, by our silences as well as our words, by our choices, gestures and attitudes. We may not always do it well, but we always do it. (Unknown)

Is Erin being difficult or is she experiencing difficulties?

As an example of a young child with speech and language problems, you may want to think about Erin's experiences of a day in your setting. Does the ethos and organization of the setting mean that her needs are being met? Are the activities being differentiated and are there, for example, visual prompts to help her navigate her way around?

Is Erin able to make choices in her learning and are there routines in place so that she is becoming more confident and familiar with them?

Does her key person have realistic expectations of what she can and can't do, based on knowledge of child development and the EYFS?

Does Erin show any indications of feeling part of a community and how can you help her to interact with other children and make choices in her learning?

Does her key person understand her particular areas of difficulty and know strategies to support her and her parents? Erin may be at risk of switching off because she can't understand or communicate.

Activity:

Think about a child you are responsible for and consider the following:

- How do you speak about her and to her? If she is struggling with verbal communication, she may be looking more closely than you realize to try and work out what you mean by how you are saying it rather than what you are saying. Your body language may be expressing more than you would like it to! Be aware of whether what you are saying matches how you look. You may intend your words to be calm, but your facial expression or body language may be giving a contradictory message.

- Do you model and encourage good listening skills?

- How often do you smile and acknowledge the child positively?

- How much time do you spend communicating with the child? How could you improve this?

- Do you place enough emphasis on listening rather than talking, waiting rather than anticipating and prompting too quickly?

- When do you need to support the child most and which activities does she enjoy most?

- How well do you think you communicate with her parents: is the communication open, inclusive and well-managed?

Positive Personal, Social and Emotional Development

Children who are experiencing difficulties with speech, language and communication may struggle to express their feelings and to understand how to communicate their needs to others. This in turn can have a significant effect on their ability to build good relationships with others and to use social skills effectively. Communication and behaviour problems are often found together. It's important to think about how these affect one another when looking for ways to improve a child's daily experiences as behaviour is a form of communication which we can interpret.

Personal, Social and Emotional Development (PSED) underpins all aspects of a child's experiences and development. They are seen by the DCSF as three building blocks of future successes in life and they form one of the six areas of learning and development. They are closely linked to each other and consist of:

- Self awareness: understanding who we are.

- Social awareness: understanding ourselves in relation to others.

- Emotional awareness: understanding our own feelings and those of others.

This is seen as such a high priority that the Childcare Act 2006 places a duty on local authorities (LAs) with their partners in settings 'to improve the well-being of all young children in their area and to reduce the inequalities between them'. (Source: DCSF: Social and Emotional Aspects of Development: Guidance for EYFS practitioners: 2008 00707-2008BKT-EN)

Self-esteem

If a child is struggling to communicate with others for whatever reason, they are less likely to develop self-confidence and to be able to make friendships with others.

Self-esteem refers to how we feel about ourselves and whether this is positive or negative. Children who have low self-esteem are more likely to have negative feelings about themselves and there is evidence

that older primary aged children with SLCN see themselves more negatively in terms of how well they do in school, how well they are accepted socially, and how they behave. Although this may not seem so apparent in younger children, it is disturbing to think of the consequences of long-term language difficulties which are not resolved.

The key-person approach helps children to settle in their setting and provides consistent care and emotional support to enable the child to 'blossom'. The EYFS stresses that it is now a specific legal requirement for each child to be assigned a key person. In childminding settings this is the childminder.

Some of the areas that the key person will be significant in delivering are:

- Ensuring that the child feels safe both physically and emotionally, and is helped to make secure attachments.

- Helping the child feel that they belong by having routines and rituals, for example, welcome and departure songs and greetings.

- Helping children to label and recognize their feelings.

- Helping children to cope with their fears and anxieties.

Summary

The impact of SLCN can be felt across a wide range of areas:

- Literacy: Difficulties with reading and spelling, as well as difficulty in ordering thoughts and using appropriate grammar and content.

- Learning: Much information is communicated verbally and this means children will experience difficulties with understanding and acquiring vocabulary and concepts, such as shape and number.

- Social Interaction: Children can become fearful, shy and unwilling to build social relationships and friendships. They experience difficulties with understanding the thoughts and feelings of others and may upset other children by their inappropriate use of language. They may be wrongly labeled as behaviour problems if they seem consistently to ignore instructions given to groups of children. They may withdraw and this kind of behaviour may be missed because the child isn't making a fuss. This can be a cause of concern and is often a strategy that girls may use.

How can the setting support the child?

Dukes and Smith (2009) identify a five step model to recognizing additional needs which stresses the importance of communicating with others:

1. A holistic view: think about what you already know about the child. Talk with parents.

2. Reflect on your own setting and practice: what is the child's experience of a day in your setting? Talk with other staff.

3. Think about what is developmentally appropriate for the child, taking into account their age and stages of development.

4. Focus on the child's areas of strength and concern. Involve other practitioners if possible in making several targeted observations of the child and analyze them.

5. Decide on a 'plan, do, and review' cycle of action and seek further advice (with parental permission).

Be:

• Explicit.

• Clear.

• Consistent.

• Use gesture and intonation to support verbal instructions.

• Speak slowly after you have gained the child's attention using their name. It's important also not to turn your head away from the child during the time you are communicating with them.

• Try to maintain a relaxed facial expression as the child will quickly pick up on any signs of frustration.

• Give one instruction at a time and leave time for the child to carry this out, allowing more time for processing the information and instructions. Visual prompts such as photos, drawings and gestures can be used in the context of practical activities to support learning and to support listening. Having defined spaces for activities is really useful - these can be labeled: the puzzle table, the paint and brushes, the home corner - and also supported with symbols or pictures to reinforce the area and activity.

• Talk about things that can be seen, and use everyday events to develop vocabulary: are they putting on a 'top' or a 'sweater'?

• Allow the child to choose when they want to tell you something: look and sound interested in what they are engaged in.

• Identify resources you know the child is really attracted to, such as TV characters.

• Avoid finishing what they are trying to say, but maintain interest: its 'the power of the pause'.

Find time to listen and talk with the child on an individual basis so that you can learn to tune into their speech. Lindon (2008) points out that problems

have arisen in some early years provision when practitioners are under pressure to meet targets and gather evidence. As a result, some teams or individuals may lack confidence in justifying time spent in 'just' talking with children. Children however learn about words, sentence structure and use of language through relaxed, one to one interactions with friendly, familiar adults who model good language structure and content and this needs to be a high priority.

Provide shared contexts such as photo-books, play activities and well-known story books to help predict the content of the conversation. Using photographs of the child, their family and significant people can help to support conversations. If children find it hard to say people's names, they can show the photographs and provide a context for the conversation.

Using routine and structure: children often need help in learning the nursery routines, but knowing these routines will then provide a good deal more security. It is helpful to lead children through routines like 'Coats on and off' or 'What happens at snack time', demonstrating and using simple language to describe what is happening. Using a photo book to represent the nursery activities can be a great help for children who are unable to express where they want to go and play.

Model and emphasize the correct versions of words rather than asking the child to repeat words. Expand what they have said by repeating it with a little more detail: 'Cat there' is repeated by the adult as: 'Yes the cat is over there'.

Can you use your interpretation of the child's gestures and facial expressions: Can you 'read' their faces and actions?

Identify and prioritize key vocabulary.

Use picture sequences to develop sequencing skills and then encourage them to say something about each picture which creates a simple but coherent story.

What is good listening?

- Listening to others, using our ears and waiting our turn: (model showing respect).

- Looking at who is talking.

- Thinking about the words we are using.

- Sitting quietly and comfortably.

(Adapted from Garforth 2009)

Pepper and Weitzmann (2004) have proposed some useful strategies for practitioners and parents:

The Four S's

Say less, use short sentences to avoid overload and confusion.

Stress the most important word in the sentence: the pan is HOT.

Slow speech down with a short pause between words.

Show, point and add gestures.

SPARK

When playing a game, song, a rhyme or a routine:

Start the same way every time, using a picture as a prompt.

Plan each child's turn so that they can anticipate what comes next.

Adjust the routine if necessary so that a child understands when it is their turn.

Repeat the same actions/ words each time as this develops a sense of security.

Keep the end the same so that the children feel secure.

Music and Movement

Movement is a child's first language. It is the means by which children come to understand the world around them. It is the basis of communication, language, sensory integration, learning and living (Goddard Blythe, 2008). The Practice Guidance for the Early Years Foundation Stage (2008) recognizes that 'all children learn best through activities and experiences that engage all the senses. For example, music, dance, rhymes and songs play a key role in language development'. The guidance also reinforces the importance of encouraging children to communicate their thoughts, ideas and feelings through a range of expressive forms including body movement and dance.

Wings of Childhood (Lazarev, 2007) is a collection of songs written to inspire movement and development in young children from three to seven years of age and can be used to improve children's attention, balance and coordination and help them to get 'ready' for school. The song collection can be used for singing activities or as the basis for a music and movement programme. The animal characters were specially selected to support research on early childhood movement and they can help prepare children by laying good foundations for more advanced academic skills. Studies following the progress of children whose mothers have used the programme have shown that the children have improved coordination and language skills. The songs, such as *The Turtle*, can be used as an enjoyable singing activity to develop rhythm, memory and singing together. The same song can also be used alongside a simple movement, creeping in time to the music.

For children with SLCN, resources like these can be a useful way to provide a wide range of sound and movement activities which are also linked to a simple story. Current research has highlighted the significance of the child's listening environment (three to five years) in acquiring language skills, speech and later reading. Singing along aids their sound discrimination. Children are encouraged to express the music with their whole bodies: through running, skipping, jumping, rolling and balancing.

Whilst recognizing the importance of music, it is best used thoughtfully and not as background wallpaper, as this can be irritating or distracting for children who are struggling with overloaded sensory input. Music can however be used very effectively to support specific activities. Many practitioners will know the value and fun to be experienced through singing as children can learn to listen for the music starting and stopping, clapping rhythms, taking turns and learning repetitive actions and words.

The sounds of language vary according to whether we are reading, singing or speaking. The more experience children have with language in all these forms, the better they will become at discriminating the various sounds of language and the wider vocabulary they will be able to understand and use with confidence. Singing songs and reciting chants play a valuable role in laying the foundation for reading readiness, as well as communication in the broader context. Songs, chants and rhymes help develop listening skills and thinking skills, as well as providing experience of sharing with others.

Children who have difficulty interacting with their peers are sometimes aggressive and uncontrolled, with the result being that other children avoid them, or they are sometimes so timid that they voluntarily withdraw from others. Music can have special benefits for children in each of these groups.

When we share nursery rhymes with children, some might criticize this as being irrelevant in the modern age, but I would prefer to think of this as linking us to traditions in the past and providing a source of rich vocabulary. Children need experience of a wide range of culturally diverse experiences which value their own and other cultures. A sense of rhythm helps develop the flow of movement and speech, as well as a love of music and singing for the joy of it. Nursery rhymes help to develop pre-literacy skills, such as awareness of phonics.

Visual and auditory sequencing skills allow us to remember, in the correct order, information we have seen or heard. This is needed for the more advanced skills such as spelling words, as well as sequencing day to day activities. We expect children to learn and follow sequences all the time and this can be very frightening for the child who cannot understand or is unable to organize this information for whatever reason. Singing can lighten your mood, make you feel happier and boost your memory.

Marlene Rattigan (2007) has produced some lovely music and movement activities for children, try these with your children:

This first one is very simple, but very good for both physical development and for helping children to learn sequences:

Over The Ocean

Pre-teach the actions. This seems like such as simple activity, but it can be surprisingly difficult for the young children to master.

They roll one arm over the other (roly poly arms) in a forward direction for the first part.

For 'jellyfish', put fingertips together and push palms together and apart in a rhythmical fashion to simulate a jellyfish swimming.

Repeat the rhyme, rolling forearms backwards.

For the 'starfish' in the second verse; make your hands into fists, then open them wide twice, quickly.

Over the ocean, over the sea,
Catching jellyfish for my tea.

Over the ocean, over the sea,
Catching starfish just for me.

I Hide My Hands: Marlene Rattigan

I hide my hands (Put them behind your back)
I shake my hands
I give a little clap
I shake my hands
I hide them in my lap
I creep my hands (Fingers walking up the body)
I crawl my hands
Right up to my nose
I creep my hands
I crawl my hands
Way down to my toes

(Helps with fine-motor coordination, memory of sequences, body awareness and directionality.)

Movement Fun

- Finger play exercises and rhymes

- Clapping simple patterns and rhythms

- Using simple home-made shakers, jingle bells and drums

- Ribbons and streamers on short sticks can be used to develop language concepts: big movements, little movements, wave/shake/wiggle etc

- Rolling along the floor slowly: different ways of rolling, rolling along to land on a cushion, talking about our arms, legs, knees and elbows!

- Crawling along the floor and around a course

Games and Activities to Develop Articulation Skills (moving the mouth and tongue)

Note: Be alert to signs of fatigue as the muscles can tire very quickly, and stop before it becomes a chore.

The lips are important for control of dribbling, swallowing and blowing, as well as making sounds. The tongue is important for chewing, licking and swallowing and plays a major role in producing speech sounds.

Blowing or sucking games with different kinds of straws:

- Blow boats across a bowl of water, blow bubbles and blow simple musical instruments such as whistles.

- Blow ping-pong balls across a table or along the floor.

- Blow through different sized pipes which will help make a rounded shape for the mouth, and encourages the child to use their lips only, not teeth as well.

- Make faces in a mirror together.

- Lick lollipops, and cooking spoons.

- Try licking sideways, upwards behind the teeth, downwards onto the chin.

Games to develop Language, Vocabulary and Memory

Shopping Game

What you need:

- Shopping bag
- Small group of children
- A few familiar 'shopping' items such as a book, a comb, some fruit

Instructions:

I am working in the shop. (Flat palm to chest).
And this is what I say. (Hand touches mouth and gestures forward).

Good morning to you. (Insert child's name here and wave to them).

What will you buy today?

The named child then selects two items and names them as she puts them in the bag.

Then ask the children to recall what she has put in the bag and then take these items out (in the same order) and replace in the centre.

Repeat the game with the next child.

Increase to three or four items, depending on the child.

Awareness of Sound

Use listening walks where you focus on noticing what you can hear: loud noises, quiet noises, vocabulary to describe sounds.

Messy Play

Tracey Beckerleg's (2009) book *Fun with Messy Play: Ideas and Activities for Children with Special Needs* is a lovely resource to explore language through activities which help to relax muscles, develop gross and fine motor skills, social play and turn taking, concentration, body awareness and communication skills.

There are obvious health and safety issues to take into account when working with foodstuffs and there should be clear guidance on how these activities are managed.

Tinned tomatoes: poke, squeeze, pat, scoop.

Baked beans: scoop, pour, squeeze, smell, move around.

Jelly: squeeze, poke, scoop, pour, explore.

Non-messy play can be achieved through using the same ingredients in plastic zipped bags, where the child can see the contents and poke, prod, pat and talk about them to stimulate language and vocabulary development.

In messy play, singing can be used to accompany movement and to encourage language and communication skills. Eye contact is essential for language and communication development and by sitting opposite a child, you can take opportunities to catch and positively react to any possible eye contact opportunities. You can also imitate the movements of the child to encourage them to mimic you.

Informal Activities

Encourage children to join you in simple activities such as shelling peas. The child can sit and watch, observe in passing or choose to join in as you talk together and enjoy simple conversation where the child can control their level of involvement (Tassoni 2008).

Steve Biddulph, speaking to the 'Open Eye' Conference in 2008 (http://openeyecampaign. wordpress.com), revealed that there were two striking outcomes of a large-scale project into what makes good pre-primary education:

1. Children's language performance gains decrease in proportion to the time spent in forced group academic activities.

2. They increase in proportion to the amount of time spent in free choice and expressive activities.

The implication of this is that the early years practitioners need the confidence to enrich their children's learning through a range of activities which the children positively engage with on their own terms.

Clay/Playdough

When using clay, children can play alone or engage with others at many different levels. Children often spontaneously engage in communication with others through the medium of this activity. Dough is a calming, settling activity, which aids in the development of fine motor skills (hands/fingers). It can be used for practising letter formation for four to five year olds and is non- threatening as any 'mistakes' can just be rolled away! Children can also create shapes and learn colour recognition. It offers many opportunities for engaging in conversation and the development of vocabulary relating to the cutters, rollers etc which can be experimented with.

Story Time

How often have you found yourself reading to a child or group of children and realized that they are not really with you? They may be fidgeting, or looking around, not focused on the book or on you. Becoming actively involved in the story, particularly for children who are 'wrigglers' helps them to connect with what they are being told. This can help the child with SLCN if they have opportunities to learn vocabulary through moving under, around, through in active exploration.

Using real objects to highlight characters or parts of the story can also help keep the 'wrigglers' engaged for a bit longer if they have something to hold or to take out of the story bag.

Quiet Time

As well as providing fun activities like these, it is also important to create quiet areas in the room where a child can rest and experience peace. For children who are struggling with social communication and understanding, it is important that they have opportunities to rest and recover, as the efforts they need to make can be very tiring for them. Time out is also valuable for those children who can be over-stimulated in their senses and need some time away from all the stimulation.

Organization of the Setting

Children have vast differences in the skills and experience which they bring to their setting and each setting has its unique ethnic, cultural and economic background. How a child learns is also influenced partly by their natural inclinations but also by the opportunities they are presented with. By providing a multisensory environment, where children can explore through touch, movement, listening and observing, you are developing all their learning styles. When an infant uses his or her senses to interact with the environment; novelty and curiosity are the means through which the infant brain grows and learns. Novelty and curiosity encourage movement, which is critical for the development of good physical and sensory systems which work effectively.

Creating a communication supportive environment is beneficial for all children. The Inclusion Development Plan (IDP) from the National Strategies provides extensive information about supporting children with speech, language and communication needs in the EYFS. Below are some of the points they outline which relate to reflecting on your daily practice.

As a practitioner do you...

• Work with colleagues (where appropriate) to ensure that you are providing experiences which are stimulating, nurturing and positive?

• Know which children in your group are attending other settings or receiving support to develop their speech, language and communication skills from other professionals?

• Use specific words, signs or symbols to indicate that you want them to listen?

• Value and acknowledge children's non-verbal communications and reflect on your own non-verbal communication skills?

As a SENCO do you...

• Ensure there is a consistent approach to a child's learning at home and in the setting/between settings?

As a leader or manager do you...

• Know where parents can go in their local areas to attend support groups or courses on speech, language and communication development, and share this information with parents?

• Make links with other settings, and share information about children who attend more than one setting.

Signing

Children using a support for communication development, such as a signing system, need reminding to look carefully and focus on the signs being used. There are a number of signing or symbol systems available and the practitioners most in contact with the child need to develop a good level of proficiency in using the system. It is also helpful if other children learn some of the signs to help in communicating.

Dummies

Advice from the IDP is that sucking dummies and bottles can have an impact on a child's speech and language development and policy in settings should reflect this. The reasons given are that children who suck dummies have fewer opportunities to practice and develop the skills needed for clear speech and they make fewer sounds. They also refer to a risk of the child learning distorted patterns of speech because the teat prevents normal mouth movements. It is recognized that a child may need a dummy when upset or as part of their sleep routine. Even this should be phased out as soon as possible. However, there are other reasons that dummies and bottles are still being used by older toddlers, which can be related to parental priorities and child care experience.

How can the setting support the parents/carers?

A sound working relationship with the parents/carers is essential for all children and particularly when there are concerns about development. Parents may feel guilty about leaving their child in the early years setting and it is important that they are confident that their child's needs will be met effectively. When a child has communication difficulties, parents are even more likely to have a raised level of concern and will need reassuring that the practitioners can meet their child's needs sympathetically and with clear plans of action.

The Bercow Report

In 2008 the government announced a £52 million package to tackle communication problems. This came as a result of the independent review by John Bercow, MP, commissioned by the government. Among its recommendations was the advice for parents to help their child develop communication skills by sharing activities like family meals and outings with conversation as the focus. Early intervention was seen as vital and the Every Child a Talker programme aims to support early years' practitioners in this.

Parents should know their child better than anyone else, but they may be reluctant to ask if you think their child has difficulties. On the other hand, they may be seeking support and guidance in how they can help at home. When practitioners can establish an open relationship with parents which is focused on the welfare of the child, an atmosphere of mutual respect is established. They are often the first to notice difficulties as they interact with other children with apparently more advanced skills.

Many parents will carry their own experiences of childhood within them and these can have a profound influence on how they behave as a parent. Not all parents have had a good role model to follow and they are limited in their knowledge of what to expect and how to deal with difficulties may be limited. They may not feel confident to deal with their child, particularly if the child is experiencing problems which they do not know how to deal with manage effectively. Parents are, however, in most circumstances, the child's first educator and establishing constructive relationships with them can have a positive impact on the child's day--to day living and long-term potential for achievement and wellbeing.

Families

The EYFS stresses the importance of recognizing the diversity of family relationships and structures. This is seen as a first step to supporting equality and inclusion.

Children may live with one parent or both, or may live with other significant adults.

There may also be cultural differences which have an ongoing effect on how parents perceive their child's behaviour and progress in relation to what they expect of their child and what their extended family may be expecting of them. Finding out about individual and cultural expectations is therefore an important part of the practitioner's role.

More than one language may be spoken at home and this can increase the difficulties a child may experience with developing effective communication. However, it is also important for the child to develop and maintain the language which is dominant in the home environment, as this is where the child spends more of their time. Opportunities should be given for children to express themselves in their home language for some of the time. Further guidance on this is available in the National Strategies booklet: *Supporting children learning English as an additional language* (Ref: 00683-2007BKT-EN)

Some Key Strategies

When a child is experiencing communication difficulties, it may be useful to have some information from parents about when their child reached various milestones, such as early feeding, sitting unaided, crawling and walking.

Checks

Have the parents talked with the health visitor and/or doctor regarding any concerns relating to speech, language and communication?

- Has the child's hearing been checked?

- Is there a family history of related difficulties?

- Have there been repeated ear infections which may have had a long-term effect on the efficiency of their hearing?

- Understanding what the child is trying to communicate: how is this dealt with at home?

- And what does mum/dad/auntie do? Knowing if there are any special signs/gestures the parent and child use when the child is feeling sick or unwell: what should you be looking for?

Meetings with Parents

Before the meeting

What evidence or observations do you need to have prepared before the meeting?

When meeting with parents, it is helpful if there is a private place to speak and, if a record is made of the meeting, copies of which are made available to all involved.

You may already have developed a record format for this. If so, check that it covers the following areas:

Date and reason for the meeting
This should also include who attended the meeting and who called for the meeting to take place.

Summary of the discussion
Keeping a record of meetings will show that you are reflecting on the quality of your provision and

will also enable you to track any changes and development over time.

Try to summarize the points briefly rather than lengthy paragraphs and, if possible, agree these at the time so that there is no later misunderstanding. Avoid using jargon and abbreviations which parents may not understand.

Parental consent for referral
If you feel that a child needs referral to a specialist support service such as Speech and Language Therapy, you do need parental consent. It is possible that the parents will not feel able to accept this recommendation, even when you provide them with targeted evidence to support your concern. Some parents find it very difficult to accept that their child has any difficulties or delay and there may be a number of reasons for this which lie outside your scope of influence.

By pointing out that early identification and extra support can sometimes prevent longer term problems, you may be able to persuade them that this is an appropriate action. Difficulties in talking, listening, literacy and other subject areas, as well as making friends may become more persistent if not addressed as early as possible. If parents are still unwilling to give consent, this needs to be recorded and raised again at the next review when family circumstances may have changed.

Action points
It is generally accepted that targets are more likely to be successfully implemented if they follow the SMART structure below:

Specific
Measurable
Achievable
Realistic
Time-related

Review date
The review date will depend on the reasons for the meeting and the action points agreed.

Sharing Ideas with Carers
Sharing ideas and understanding with parents is part of the role of a helpful practitioner. At the same time, it is part of your role to support parents in the identification of difficulties and to resist pressure to move their child on at a developmentally inappropriate pace. By showing what you are doing and having confidence in your practice, you can respond to parents who may have unrealistic expectations:

Young children need to feel valued for who they are. Their development unfolds because they are encouraged and allowed to relish what they are learning at the moment. Four-year-olds need to have been enabled to enjoy being three-year-olds, five-year-olds need to have spent time being unharrassed four-year-olds. (Lindon J (2008) *What Does it mean to be Three?* Revised Edition. Step Forward Publishing.)

Ask questions such as 'Do you want water or juice?' This is easier for the child to respond to than, 'What do you want to drink?' as the words they need to use are already provided.

Keep a box of everyday objects such as a hairbrush or cup. Each day select an item and use it, saying the word at the same time: 'Here is your red cup. We can pour your milk into the cup'. Use gestures at the same time and get eye contact before you start. Make sure you repeat the words rather than: 'Here is your red cup, we can pour milk in it.' Children need repetition if they are to receive overlearning necessary for their language development. Some children will understand after three to five repetitions, whereas a child with SLCN may need to see/hear something many, many more times in order to learn it.

Children often attempt to involve their parents in pretend play. Playing alongside their children, parents can model play activities and this allows them to participate in a dialogue free of the pressures of 'real' communication. This gives the parents and the child freedom to experiment with different communication styles and roles.

Sing lullabies and nursery rhymes, linked to gentle rocking rhythms which also stimulate the sense of touch.

When telling a story, act it out with different voices to help keep attention.

Use actions and finger rhymes.

Use picture cards/photos of things around the house and play games with these.

Kids Fiz Biz games (see resource section).

Television

Watching television can be very helpful for stressed and overworked parents and carers, and there are many suitable programmes for children of all ages. When possible, (even if only occasionally) parents should try to watch with their children and talk about what is going on. At the end of the programme talking about it and acting some of it out can be a valuable shared experience.

Transition to School

When a child starts primary school, it is possible that teachers and other staff will have limited specialist knowledge of working with a child with SLCN. This does mean that this can be a time of great stress for parents as this is where the pre-school setting can play a major role in ensuring that the child's needs are understood and met effectively. Children need to have their unique patterns of strengths and weaknesses understood and, at the same time, teachers need to be informed early on in the transition process. This collaborative approach of 'team around the child' is central to the Every Child Matters (ECM) ethos.

Children with SLCN are at a great disadvantage in primary schools, compared to many other children in their class and in the school as a community. SLCN is a hidden disability in many respects and as such, it is not always easy for the school to understand or manage. Parents often feel that they have to act as their child's champion when fighting for the adaptations that are needed for their child to learn with less stress and more success. Academic achievement will be hard to attain as well as developing social relationships and conforming to behavioural expectations.

Final Thoughts

Unlike a child with a broken arm or leg in a cast, the child with communication difficulties is not immediately identifiable as in need of additional or differentiated support. As their difficulties may also be associated with other long-term consequences, such as social and emotional problems, attention deficit and delayed fine and gross motor skills, prioritizing where to start can be daunting. Reflecting on one or two children you work with every day, what two changes could you make straight away that would make a real difference to their experiences with you on a daily basis? Which of the resources listed would be of most value to you in achieving this? How confident do you feel now in identifying children who may have communication difficulties. A planning sheet has been included for recording this.

References and resources

Beckerleg T (2009) *Fun with Messy Play*. Jessica Kingsley Publishers, London and Philadelphia

Delamain C, Spring J (reprinted 2009) *Achieving Speech and Language Targets*. Speechmark Publishing Limited, Milton Keynes
This book is aimed at practitioners working with children who have significant language delay and who are in their first year of school. As such, it sits outside the age range of this book, but has many useful checklists, games and resources to develop a greater understanding of speech, language and communication issues.

DCSF (2008) *Practice Guidance for the Early Years Foundation Stage*. DCSF ref: 00266-2008BKT-EN

David T, Gooch K, Powell, S Abbott L (2003) *Birth to Three Matters: A Review of the Literature*. DfES Research Report Number 444

Dukes C, Smith M (2009) *Recognizing and Planning for Special Needs in the Early Years*. Sage Publications, London
This practical handbook has been written by two area Senco's with extensive early years' experience. It has been praised as 'the ultimate resource for busy practitioners, who want good, clear advice on what to look for and how to set up necessary provision'. It includes case studies, sample policies and a number of photocopiable resources on a CD. It links to the EYFS, emphasizing its 'holistic child' principles.

Garforth S (2009) *Attention and Listening in the Early Years*. Jessica Kingsley Publishers, London and Philadelphia
In this very useful book, Sharon Garforth provides a practical course designed for groups of children aged two to four. Each group session is planned a round a theme such as 'The Farm' or 'The Zoo'. It arose out of her desire to encourage and develop children's attention and listening skills so that they have a better chance of achieving their potential in communication, speech and language skills and, consequently, their learning skills. It includes activities which require children to practice turn taking, responding to their name, performing actions such as singing or shaking instruments and matching sounds.

Goddard-Blythe SA (2008) *What Babies and Children Really Need*. Hawthorn Press, Stroud

Lazarev M (2007) *Wings of Childhood*. Available from www.inpp.org.uk

Lindon J (2008) *What does it mean to be three (revised edition)*. Step Forward Publishing, London

Peer L (2005) *Glue Ear: An essential guide for teachers, parents and health professionals*. David Fulton Publishers, London

Pepper J, Weitzman E (2004) *It Takes Two to Talk*. The Hanen Centre

Rattigan M (2007) *Kidz-fiz-biz: physical business for kids: learning through drama, dance and song*. Crown House Publishing
Marlene Rattigan is an inspirational writer and workshop presenter. Her books are packed full of practical ways to develop verbal and non-verbal communication.

Tassoni P (2008) *Penny Tassoni's Practical EYFS Handbook*. Heinemann, Essex

Talking Time Resources, University of Michigan, Department of Psychology: *Obstacles in Early Childhood Development*

Resources

MacLachlan H. *Let's Talk with Under 5s Handouts*. www.elklan.co.uk
This contains 70 pages full of ideas to encourage speaking, listening and language skills of all under fives. The handouts are ideal for parents, childminders and early years practitioners wanting some basic skills and knowledge. This is available from the website above.

Singing Hands: It's Signing Time. This DVD introduces Makaton signing through fun sessions. Babies naturally use gestures such as pointing and waving and in this programme the signs are used together with speech and in English word order. The DVD includes favourite songs such as 'Wind the Bobbin Up', 'Incy Wincy Spider' and 'If You're Happy and You Know It'. www.singinghands.co.uk

DCSF Publications: There are many publications available for download and to order. Tel: 08456022260

Libraries

Local libraries can offer expert advice and activities for pre-school children. Pre-school children can experience language through shared rhymes and story-telling, and staff can advise on good quality, free reading materials. Support from librarians can help parents to become more confident in sharing books with their children.

Web-Sites

The following sites provide useful information:

www.afasic.org.uk
Afasic produces booklets, leaflets, newsletters as well as training, workshops and works with local and central government to improve education and support for children with speech, language and communication difficulties. It supports research projects and works with other organizations.

Afasic also runs courses and activities for children and young people to support them at times of transition. This helps reduce their social isolation and to develop their communication skills.

www.inpp.org.uk

www.talktoyourbaby.org.uk

www.talkingpoint.org.uk

www.ican.org.uk

www.kidshealth.org.nz

www.movetolearn.com.au

Mary Mountstephen can be contacted at:
mem@imaginationgym.ws or via her web-site: www.multisensoryinterventions.co.uk